I0151468

Every Girl Becomes the Wolf

poems by

Laura Madeline Wiseman
&
Andrea Blythe

Finishing Line Press
Georgetown, Kentucky

Every Girl Becomes the Wolf

ACKNOWLEDGMENTS

Grateful appreciation is expressed to the editors and staff of the following
journals and anthologies in which many of these poems were first accepted
and appeared:

"The Hellos from the Corners of Quiet Rooms" and "Holding the Keys,"
Quail Bell Magazine
"Inside Her Curious White Sleigh," Rock the Chair Weekly Poetry
Challenge, *Yellow Chair Review*
"Hunger," *Rose Red Review*
"A Gathering of Baba Yagas," *Strange Horizons* and *They Said: A Multi-Genre
Anthology of Contemporary Collaborative Writing*
"Lighting the Ghost Lamps," *The Drowning Gull*
"The Path That Cuts through Famine," *Silver Blade*
"A Wake of Crepuscular Ruin," *Linden Avenue Literary Journal*
"Stone Clutched to Chest," *Star*Line*
"The Red Inside of Girls," *Nasty Women Poets: An Unapologetic Anthology of
Subversive Verse*

Publisher: Leah Maines
Editor: Christen Kincaid
Cover Art: "A Good Milking" by Katy Horan
Author Photos: Laura Madeline Wiseman & Andrea Blythe
Cover Design: Elizabeth Maines McCleavy

Printed in the USA on acid-free paper.
Order online: www.finishinglinepress.com
also available on amazon.com

Author inquiries and mail orders:
Finishing Line Press
P. O. Box 1626
Georgetown, Kentucky 40324
U. S. A.

Table of Contents

Lighting the Ghost Lamps

The luminescent moonlight lilts with hope
as we climb your lamp-lit drive. Please, open your door,
lead us inside the hall, and greet us with dusty kisses.
Our bones are cold. We're forgetting to bleed. Upstairs
one summer you taught us the ache of want,
the ease of forget in heat. Your porch lamp ghosts,

barely brightens our own whispering ghosts—
our hands tattooed in interstellar swirls, comet tails. We hope
you accept transparency, unveiling space. We want
offerings—guttering candles, creaky chains and doors,
dark shadows, mists—all the artistry of hauntings in upstairs
rooms where curtains skirt the floors to fall like kisses.

Each chilling draft here is more than a draft, a kiss
returned, some years, some centuries late. We ghost,
half-lost, half-wandering in the labyrinth of upstairs
rooms of storage space, beds draped in sheets. We hope
you illuminate the silver key in your heart and find the door.
You are made of bones and air, we of stars. We want

to fall into you, meteor bright and burning. We want
flesh, the electric pulse of hushed, corporeal kisses,
your body pressing us against the frame of the door.
Table-turning in the stage of your room, will our ghosts
flicker like lamps, waver with the memory of past hope?
Or will you hold us in that glowing space upstairs,

where we once circled you like moons, upstairs
where a telescope waits to see the planets—Venus' want,
Mars' fury, Mercury's need to wander? We never hoped
for eclipse, for the shadowy erasure of your kiss,
for the full moon haunt of lonely hours. We want
to swell into existence, to give up being ghostly,
be what we couldn't on that blue night. Open your door,

pass through this long hallway of more doors,
and find us gazing upon the moonlight dust among stairs
that lead to galaxy swirls, nebula ghosting
through noctilucent skies. Find our wantings
among your bone-cold embrace, your deathly kiss.
Such travelers as us are encumbered by hopes.

Every door closes upon unclaimed wants,
while upstairs we feign presence, fake kisses,
ghost touch, discover the celestial weight of hope.

The Hellos from the Corners of Quiet Rooms

They cavort through tombstones in skinny jeans, Converse high tops, and Ray-Bans to play at conjuring ghosts. They imitate the '80s, but they weren't there. They never saw *Poltergeist*, never the flicker of afterlife—silverware bending on its own, chairs sliding across the floor by forces unseen, voices speaking from distant spaces, or mirrors glittering in the night. *Even now TVs make me cringe*, I tell one. Then to another, *When I visit my sister, I stay at hotels, and I always drape towels over the screens.* They laugh, skipping over a freshly dug grave. Why did I agree to meet them here? One tosses faux flowers. Another twirls faded pinwheels. When my sister bought an old farmhouse, one room became her wardrobe. Among the antique mirrors, she placed ankle-length skirts, leather kid gloves, parasols. Every time the door slammed shut, children's hands touched her ankles or shook lacy slips. *They're harmless*, she said, though other things bothered her—the boarded up windows, the attic that groaned with the wind, the room with the peeling closet doors. When he beat her over the money he lost and then left her, she rented that room to strangers who became the kind of friends who pounded walls, remained in the kitchen after midnight, left hotline numbers tucked behind her coffee cups. I brought my sister comfort in the form of old movies, the kind that crept under the skin, then stayed with her late into the dark. How many times does it take until a film fuses with the psyche? The fuzz of static hisses when palms press against screens. *Hellos* echo in the rooms my sister knew as hell. *They're here.* Others may leave, but some cannot, sometimes even kin. I learned to sleep alone, clutching a pillow against shadowed corners and empty doorways. I jump when objects fall, my eyes snapping open, feeling the trace of their hands whisper against limbs slipped from sheets. I never again stayed with my sister after that last time. Who would? Alone, she sings lullabies for children spirits well past midnight. Others bring Ouija boards, gazing balls, or candles as if an invitation is needed. It's these I meet in the cemetery now, the ones who want to visit the home my sister refused to leave. Would they even see what presses from every opening there? Every home has such secrets, foundations built over what should never have been maimed—no escape, just a move into another set of flickering rooms, then the wait for the *Hello*.

A Music of Shattering Ice

Never mind the wind, cutting through shirt and skin   to bone,
or the bite of frostnip freezing skin to numb, the itch and pain,

the red patches on fingers and toes. It's the keening
that carves,   like a glacier grinding,   an unending wail.

Her body is more solid than flesh. Her scream burns, as though
her voice can cross   these shimmering mounds.

You tell me frostburn is only second degree if it blisters,
blackens, hardens. Muscles, tendons, vessels, and nerves freeze.
        Remember that time-traveler in Chicago who lost his feet?

Her hair whips, lashing the blue of her face. Her howl constant,
a chanting song.   No amount of fleece or down will preserve heat
or stop hypothermia.   Why did we come? Was it for the ice

glittering in ravines or forming crystals within our blood?
        You've become so hard I could shatter you, reassemble edges
until you resemble the shape of this place, heavy with sleet,

headwind, and bite.   Her voice knells—melody demands supplication.
Is it a warning or a fairy foresight?   Do we need a lukewarm bath,
a blanket, a doctor's knife?   My fingers can't warm,   no matter

how you cup them.   Do you remember when her screech shattered
the window pane or how sure you were that   she stood beside you
washing blood from clothes?   I used to think we could build fire

in each other. But when I reach to touch your face, you   float away.
What gusts us apart?   Home is a thing of silence.   Her singing

is unhurried, perpetual. Is she some fell creature or us?   It's said you feel
a false heat before you freeze.   What if I followed her voice into

the blinding white?   Would you even notice the warm
space between   us slip   wide and grow cold?

Would I?

Hunger

Go, they said, to where the rocks hang, jagged and sharp,
where we could walk for miles without car sounds, without
the violent honking rush of the city and its constant needs of buy
and get and more, no big boxes or chain strips or WiFi.

Go, they said, to where rocks hide, buried in dirt, hidden in water,
where we can feel, let our toes slide, listen for the cascade of stones
tumbling over like minutes falling, like breadcrumbs, like lives.

We go to where the grotto offers its opening, a dark chamber,
an oven, or maybe a house, wet with melting drip of frost
and iron-streaked, like caramel or chocolate, or a kind of sweetness.
The witch is here, we say and enter holding hands.

We come expecting terror, hungering for the thrill of this leaving,
this arrival. *Go*, our parents said, but she said, *Stay
with me. You're welcome at my hearth.* We shelter here,
my brother inside her cage, glutting on glazed donuts, sugar-sprinkled
bread, men made of ginger. I sweep up the ashes, saving the bones.

Inside Her Curious White Sleigh

My mother said she had a glass heart, too easy to shatter. She lied.
She is a snow queen made of ice, eyes glassy by drink, tongue

a shard to slice through talk, a sliver chip beneath the skin.
We lived together in a glass house on a glass mountain blasted

by the winter's cold. The roads were always closed, barred by gates.
My heart is comprised of scars, flesh thickened and hardened

like a cliff face, made jagged by glacier slide and snowstorm lashings.
I used to heave heavy, clumsy stones I found on the paths

around our home, ones buried under snow, frozen to the ground,
needing a pick axe to work them free. I made piles. I made walls.

I fashioned a slingshot to aim. Her cold hard glare never shattered,
only sent splinters, a sharp rigidity, a reflection like a mirror.

I learned to see as she saw—alpine slopes, hoary stags climbing
the crags, clouds swirling with more snow, her judgment.

She said, *All this is mine.* I wondered if so, what could be mine?
The crystalline air fragmented my tongue, taught me to speak

one truth, one against love, against the color red, against the flush
of underskin burning, that fire she claimed no one wanted—

not her, not I, not men. But I wanted her touch, any flicker
of warmth along my spine, a flash of sweetness in her gaze,

something soft, wrapped in bear fur. She had none to offer.
When she passed, she left me the shiver, the snow heart, the ice.

Invocation

Everyone knew the dark clothes, jeans frayed at the cuff, sleeves
pulled low over wrists, hair that hid eyes, but they never knew
her name. She clutched a silver skull on a chain like a rosary, whispering,
praying, caressing its boney curves and sockets, the open throat

of a self-made god of death. They fear because they are still afraid
of the dark, of what they did, of filling a girl's emptiness with nightmares—
cockatrices, griffins, harpies, and sirens. They shun her, dreading
their shadows, the dark under their skin, the wetware churn of loss.

At night she opens a book, old and leatherbound, cracked by
the weight of secrets, heavy with spells she pens. She is older
than she appears. Already, she's learned to drink of strangers' sorrows,
to reshape them inside herself, by herb and chant, to splay their cards

on the table and twist into new truths. She is becoming, engendering
with darkness, curses, and catches of children's hearts like fish in nets.
With every whispered breath, she shapes herself into another hungry one,
a nameless witch, an evocation of mists and magic, chanted charms

illuminated by candled belief. With every daily grain of sand, slipping
through the hourglass, she lets herself become old, shriveled, and bent,
invisible figure, standing like a withered tree. The magic is in the living
in such a wrinkled face. The evil is in the hollow need, the aching pit.

A Gathering of Baba Yagas

I. First Sister, Sister Winter Snake

I didn't know what choked me in the Russian courtyard,
amid the drifting jeweled wisps. I came to drink our history
hidden behind iron gates, to interpret the flag fluttering
its sickle and hammer, to witness one lone cottonwood
bright in the golden-red light. *Myth*, our sister said, *Revolution*.

A weight of fingers, again, around my throat in the sunset's glow,
luminescent and ghosting. I could neither speak nor breathe,
my tongue clamped by the past's vice-grip. When the server asked,
Coffee black? I shook my head, eyes watering, hands quaking.

We know her, are her, our sister said. *We are ancient as babble—
a language withered by family truth.* Who had I believed
we were for? I held the fairy book of Baba Yaga, the one gilded
with her image—long nose, mouth to suck, teeth to cut
a heart—open in my lap. *Why do I hunger?*

II. Second Sister, Sister Moon

My little babuscha, my mother whispered to my wrinkled face,
squeezing pruney fingers and toes, mussing my hair, knowing
the cold, sharp edges of Moscow streets, how they would scour me,
how they would whet my teeth to points and shear my leg to bone,
shaping me into yet another. *Baba Yaga,* they called me in school,
skinny girl with bony shanks, hawkish nose, birdlike fingers
carving horns to cull songs. I shaped a firebird charm to wear.
Classmates stared where it jiggled, dropping feathers of ill-luck.
My name means horror, fury, torture, pain. *Baba Yaga,* we're called,
a name I was born into, grew into, am. I wobble on chicken legs,
build fences like rotting bones, live in a home on stilts that turns
in the wind. My days feel mundane—cook, sweep, grind herbs to spell,
curse, and hex, warn so many away, tend to my sisters. Snuffling,
I nestle candles in skulls. Lift my nose, sniff for Russian men.

III. Third Sister, Sister Death

One of us was naive; the good girl men would sing-speak pop songs to
over vodka, "I Will Survive" a humming drunken mumble in July sun
as music warbled from the Black Sea boardwalk of flapping tents.

One of us was compliant, letting fate grind and mash her
like dream spells of herbs worked by mortar and pestle,
she licking the limbs of men, cracking and sucking them down,
men of marrow and bone. *Are we here of our own free will?*

What answer isn't a lie? One of us was fierce, riding out the night,
a shadow's specter, refusing her mother's latching warmth,
the sweet suckle of milk-tit beyond babyhood. I cast my voice
to the moon, snarl, be the wolf bitch for the world. Who doesn't

consume to escape? I ride the pig. I dance the old men, pull
them down. *Give me secrets,* I say, *Give me your babes.*

The Vacancy Sign Is Always On

In my rocking chair   right where he left me unmoved
with my hands positioned just so, I sit. A motel offers little,
but I know I will never leave. I am bound   to this normal life,
        and Norman, my dear, good Norman—not a trace
of his father in his build, smile, or teenage groaning—could never
abandon me.   I am still as death   in this chair.

My limbs never flexed towards any kind of ease
for others. My mundane days had been   carved out
in the work of numbered rooms—bleach sheets,
clean showers, empty trash—   shadows that steal
or seal a body another night.   This chair moans.
I won't notice. I never did, holding him and stroking
his head, calling him my good boy, while I thought
of his father, of my own hands, how my fingers learned
the silk of caskets.   They know the rungs of this chair—
polished smooth.   I'd been too young for his body's pull,
cemetery mists, or hard tumbles on unsettled graves.
The rocker's legs never find peace.   The floor creaks.

There are places some refuse to enter—cellar, boiler, shed.
In the hearse, we opened up   a stillness, our bodies
shoulder to shoulder, while we lay—slow breath
until I believed. I never wanted a man like others.

Sometimes his taxidermy failed   fur and bone
rearranged   patched   twisted into a caricature,
stitches thick and showing. I   in this chair   of course,
am more finely made. Some mother's boys collect stamps.
Others find hobbies in scavenging. Boys like mine
try to preserve the world   still—bodies frozen in motion,
caught mid-leap on wood bases, or crouching as if for prey.

I don't know if he was more exhibitionist or grave robber,
adventurous or curious, as blood kin to a mortician—
the type comfortable with decay among stones
        cold lockers   bodies idly waiting their turn.
How many chairs   did we stack then   and where?

People fill spaces with their sweat and sorrow—parlors
or bedrooms or chambers within others' bodies, the way
he filled mine. I didn't fight him when he   poured himself
into me.   I never wanted this motel. Yet, I rot.
Some places house the cold blade   of a knife.

We open the doors.   We share the keys.   We turn on
the vacancy sign. Sometimes, after he has fallen asleep,
        I think of his father—the scent of funerals, cigarettes,
that sharp chemical bite.   There will never be enough
formaldehyde to quiet the whispering of ghosts.

This rocker is worn   scratched with scars
like the faces of the state patrol officers who stop by
week after   week seeking the missing—pets, teen girls,
female teachers, neighborhood women,   an explanation.
Norman nods, nervously watches their pens   twitch
across their notebooks,   then closes the door.
He turns to the calendar again, crosses off another day,
another shiver of release.   A breeze rocks my chair
I sway with the creaking.   Some things never end.
I have my good boy and he has me.   What of

the murders in rural Wisconsin, the arrest, the monitoring?
Did it matter that I was sent away   when I began to show?
Can't an affair be quick, enough to be more kept than kin?
Could a boy shape   a family from bodies stored
in small spaces, experiments in preservation, a smell
seeping through the walls?   What matters

what others say? He had a thing about peeping guests,
but boys   will be boys. Can't everything be heard anyway?
This chair groans   a heavy weight. I smile
for him, lips positioned just so. He is my good boy.

Hidden Remains in Reflections

The value of mirrors is in the peripheral   what can be caught
in the bronze curve of a mace or the copper shine of a shield.

A queen accustoms to dangers stalking, learns to watch
in tin, lead, or a spine's gilding.   To make a mirror,

sweeten it with sugar, anoint the hard colloidal silver
with breath, exhale murmurs to deposit metal on glass.   A gift

on my wedding night from a man with a small daughter,
pale, flower-fragile—the shadowed world reflected

in her eyes.   Front-silvered, back-silvered, or silvered in gold
speak secrets to little girls' hearts, sharpened with rage, dangerous

as glass.   A mirror preserves detail, captures light, magnifies
a flaw or softens what moves steadily through shadowed trees.

To love a stranger's child, a girl with no use for me, why
did I need to question the surface?   What matters—still

water in which to peer, things of lace to bind a breast, a comb,
an apple? I ate the hart, that fibrous muscle beating,

bitter as lead. Lungs, liver, any organ lost to mountains
where one may practice alchemy to make gold or mirrors

coated in mercury.   Why did I expect her to welcome me,
clothed in drab wool, knocking, a basket heavy on my arm?

First, it was a double reflection, some vision of myself as hag,
some memory of the new queen as mother.   I walked paths

of thick woods, thorns, and twisting branches, where thieves,
outlaws, and angry girls hide from ordinary mirrors—

who wouldn't lean in to hear the silver whisper of words
that bend fair,   then murder.   Since that wedding night,

I've pressed my palms to reflections, asking for companionship,
as though love or beauty could refocus intention,   a ray

to bring some sliver of shine? Always empty,   the image
staring back at me. He was as cold as silver, she as hard.

I attended his funeral garbed in black, listened to their whispers
of poison, watched with a frozen tearless face beneath my veil.

When she fell—the red of my apple   lodged
in her throat—I let them put her in a coffin made of glass

for all to see. Visitors come to witness a fallen maiden—smeared
surface, smudged with sweaty fingers and dirty hands.

It mirrors their image, like kings, flips them,   a reversal
of perception where they are the caged—and cager—sleeping

an eternal sleep that marriage might arouse. To turn away
is an absolution, they think, safe from such kisses.

What Bodies Are Made Of

I could've stayed in the garden, fingering leaves, dipping my nose into open blooms, listening to the melody of making up a tongue, but I left. I stepped from foliage and fell. Now, it's any typical year at the county fair rib-off. I sit across from Jared, sucking ribs against my teeth. Fiery sauce drips down my hands. The picnic tables are full, curves and thick flesh, breasts like fruit to suck. So much sweeter than apples. Eve can have her bony figure, her fragile self-depreciation. Adam can have his book of names, all the things he claims, sheep, cows, me—his first wife, not his last. I long only for the snake, the whispered wisdom, the way a body can twine into darkness. Jared says I miss it—Adam, Eve, the lying upon and under, the commands. Nothing to miss. The heat of the fair ticks with insects, the whine of engines at the track, the smack of local lips, sucking their teeth. My belly strains against this dress, fabric scratching skin, the nakedness I still yearn for—just the same story played out again, and again, bodies on bodies, the succor of it. *All men are the same in the dark,* Jared once instructed, licking sap from where it dribbled. I could've stayed in Adam's shadow and let myself be eclipsed by son of a son of a son—not even son of a bitch. But I left. Now, I swallow, fueled for the sun-bright burn of pleasure and rage. I can eat all that's hidden because I opened the world, became my own round thing, picnic table scratching my thick legs, consuming rib after rib.

Walls Thick with Roots and Golden Hair

I never liked the taste of rampion. It's spinach-like leaves prickled
the tongue. Its pale carrot-like root lifted hives where I touched—but
a woman must hold fast to what she owns. The garden flourished

with belled flowers on erect stems, light hairs crawling the soil
hiding each growth. Rampion crowded out tomatoes and peppers—
more annoyance than gift. They were mine, guarded within a plot.

If wild—roads, hedges, fields—what woman wouldn't crave their bodies
to gnaw? Why beg their theft, urging husband to mount stone, if free?
She might claim it could soothe the restlessness of what swelled within,

a belief that anything could ease what inflames a throat.
What makes a woman hunger to release her burden? Her husband wept
when the child was placed in my arms as payment for theft,

while she sat passive, as if what she'd eaten didn't root out
what remained of the girl within. I couldn't help. He never thieved
the purple fists of pennyroyal or the soft spice of tansy—crimes

to forgive. Had she mistaken my garden for a witch's, each flowering
a certain use? Or did she hope to make a stolen leaf a quarrel,
a milky juice a tonic, a root a stair, a bloom an abacus to count—

He loves me? He loves me not? Did she find, once the child was gone,
an escape from his weighted shadow, a bargained solitude that comforted?
I imagine her in the quiet of her home, staking a claim to the space

around her, while I grasped the small, screaming infant, unsure
of what to do save guard her behind stone, cultivating a girl
as I had the rampion. Did we receive what we wanted? Or did we

trade burdens—child for isolation, freedom for garden? We feed
to nourish, to taste bitter and sweet, to soothe each strangle
like a long strand caught and tickling the back of the throat.

The Path that Cuts Through Famine

Loneliness is a hunger that sours the gut—but when cupboards
      hold only crumbs, a woman can endure the absence
of laughter bubbling, can usher small bodies away
      from her hearth. What matters what we strew—

white pebbles, lentils, or bread crusts? Whose lives
      are the better to starve or plumb on confections and cake?
Yesterday, I drew the paths to home in marzipan
      and then ate until I ached. Why do I never feel full?

Gingerbread cookies, peanut brownies, another scoop
      of ice cream—even sweets bitter the bored tongue.
These woods fill with hungry things like me, a want
      that guides into the underbrush,

while I crouch in preoccupation—food or children? Another meal
      for a woodcutter or the stepchildren? Birds flit. Some peck
what settles apath. Others stand as white beacons.
      In our kitchen, we have an object like a cage,

iron whorled, big enough to crawl inside. I keep my books there,
      close the door, pretend they're simple recipes to guard.
Except you, no one sits to eat what I bake—slumped shoulders, the axe
      beside the kitchen door. You rub the calluses on your hand,

lingering over the cracks. I bring you hot, sweet
      meat pie, watch your mouthfuls until you ask for more.
When you reach for me, I feel your bones—fingers, jaw,
      knobby shelf of hips. *Is there nothing to eat*

out there in the forest? I murmur against your throat, *At least we have*
      this warmth. But then, that boy and girl call out demands—
for their own warmth to consume on the porch. *Mother,*
      they say. I shudder, sense what starves inside their skin.

Their little hands, sticky fingers I am unable to bear.
    But with you, I no longer ache. I'm like a vase of jewels
and stones. Pull out any rock and worry it. Place a pin at your throat.
    Slide onto a finger a promise to soften and reshape with time.

Have you had enough yet? you ask. My answer is *never*,
        but instead, we kiss, our mouths sweet
with sugared tarts. In the morning when they've left
        with the last of the bread, I hide your axe.

A Kiss of Stone

Beauty is the sinuous coiling of snakes, a hiss like a lover's whisper,
cold stone under a palm, a freeze of foes stopped mid-action. *Hate,*

you say, *motivates looking.* My gaze is loving, calling those like you
to stay on this island of sisters. We were all once fair-cheeked temple girls

making pilgrimages to worship. Our fingers nicked by what we laid
at chiseled feet—where we first learned to love stone. We knew breakers,

the pull of tide. On Poseidon's wake, we watched ships toss, storms
bearing wreckage onto our shores. Small, mortal, we were sea-facing,

sand-loving girls who prayed to one sprung from a man's head.
We didn't know to look for the light that revealed a guise. Shimmers

around beings who, blind if unmasked. No one told us that the sweat
and muscle of mortal-bodied men like you could house lust and pain.

Temple whores, initiates, or goddesses—does it matter if we were splayed?
After it, I dragged myself from the temple, meeting no one apath—

not a sibling, fisherwoman, or friend among the wheat fields. Wobbling,
I did not hear the hiss of snakes that had become my crown. Papa turned

as I called out, *Am I still your daughter?* He looked at me and was silent.
Once among my companions, my face was fair, a feast for suitors. As girls,

we kept our sweetness among the trees. The crackle of leaves underfoot
and the scent of pine bark, sea-salt, and moss was an innocence, safe.

No gods protected us. They spurned the offerings—fresh fruit, blooms
of intertwining vines, fabric embroidered by our hands. *Is this a gift*

or my punishment? I asked the cold stone of Papa. What was this power
to quiet the hearts of men? Would it silence any breath in marble?

Now, you've come—a man bearing sword and mirror-bright shield,
accusing me of monstrousness. Do you not see the love I bear?

Your gait is a boy's strut, the swing of your shortsword a game. The blade
glints, swirling the smoke near the rafters, as you feign the final blow.

How it dreams of dressing itself in my blood. *Demon*, you call out, *Monster*.
Lover, my snakes whisper back. You hear only the hiss, a softness crawling

shivers. Your sword listens. There's a secret language weapons know,
a twin tongue of eros and thanatos—lust tangled with death.

See how your sword plunges towards me? I glide through shadows
for your sword. My snakes churn, wild with the urge to coil and strike.

We maze through my garden. Soon, we will look upon each other—
your sword stretching for the kiss, my gaze pulling you close, into stone.

The Red Inside of Girls

Every wolf sings in moonlight for his own pleasure, his own pain.
Every girl carries a basket, wears the hood of red, skips calling
out to woods dappled for adventure, for distracted wandering
in the lie of grandmother's house—her hunger, the good girl's chore.

Every girl carries a basket, wears the hood of red, skips, calling
out songs only meant to be heard by the quiet of shadows
turning the lie of grandmother's house, hunger, a girl's chore
to feed the elderly turned into a kind of seeing, how flesh rots with age

and bodies creak ancient songs heard in the house's quiet shadows.
Every girl hums her own lithe youth and becomes the wolf
feeding on the elderly, seeing with large eyes how flesh rots with age,
how the wolf opens the door, eats what rots first, swallows what

hums inside every girl, lithe with youth as she becomes the wolf.
The hunger of girls is hidden under capes and knee-length skirts as
the wolf opens the door, comely and large. He eats first what she
carries in her basket, the sweet rolls and apple cakes made

with the hunger of girls hidden under capes and knee-length skirts.
Then, they taste more, the heady fur, the pink girl flesh
carried against her basket, all sweet rolls and apple cakes, making
the room hot and sweet by devouring. The wolf hungers

for the taste of more, his heady fur sweetening pink girl flesh
as she reties the red cape, gathers her basket, closes the door to
the devouring, the room still hot and sweet. The wolf hungers
and is never sated, already longing for more girl

as she reties the red cape, gathers her basket, closes the door.
Every wolf sings in moonlight for her pleasure and her pain.
They're never sated, already longing for more. Wolves linger,
dappled in the woods of distracted adventure, for girls wanderings.

A Wake of Crepuscular Ruin

I could live with the hum of fluorescent-lit rooms, but not his smell.
It slid under doors, across my skin, slippery as mold. His voice
      jangled like tinnitus. Every word jarred my pulse. You say,

Your heart once beat for him. It was not my reaching, but his, the pressure
of his hands. An arrhythmia bloomed that couldn't be stitched
      under anesthesia. It was like I breathed through plastic,

but woke to find only his lips. You say, *You made your bed, so lie in it.*
Which beds don't lie? Which sheets aren't damp with the stench of regret?
      Last night, I slid from the window like a teen to troll the streets.

The sidewalks glittered under paper flyers, styrofoam cups, and tree litter.
Days after the election, graffiti-marked the trails, tunnels, and gutters
      with massive cocks, cunts, and curses. *It's nothing to worry about,*

you say, voice like padding. As though I've never witnessed power shifts,
the wake of damage in aftershocks. You hold my hand through shadows.
      What if I still carry him, memories stepping on my heels?

Instead, owls call. Something dashes. A car guns the silence.
You say, *I know why you're here.* Did you know he would fail to inhale
      after years of apnea? His skin clammy, but no longer blue.

No neighbor has reported the smell. No boss phoned the absence.
He never arranged a will. *They're going to say it was me,* I whisper.
      Wasn't it, in a way? you say, laughing. *You hated him enough.*

We walk. Has nothing changed? Will the windows rattle as they did
when he thundered after me? Still, I mark time in stages of decay.
      Desiccation sinks him into the bed. Flies buzz about his trunk.

He won't leave, and I can't. Even now, my body mimes him—
my hand thinning into skeletal rot, chest rasping, cheeks sagging—
      a stink that permeates, a sour sweetness on the tongue.

The Pallbearers

We carry the box towards the bucking white tent. The weight surprises our still aching arms. The mortician stands beside the open hearse while gravediggers fold hands in the lea of their truck, awaiting the cue of final words. April's cruel to the ground—a thin crust that gives under boots. Stones bloom everywhere snow weeps from the dormant grass. The service was closed casket. It's still closed now. No one wanted to see the crushing, the way her bones folded in the end. My fingers trace the clasp's nails. Are any strong enough? The cold cuts across the rows. Under the pall, the granite glimmers only when we squint. Dates march like those hours did, shadowed in spring's dusting. Earlier you told me, *I don't remember.* What if I told you, I remember only when the door shut? The wind slides damp fingers through my tights, like a whine of epigraphs, carvings, or blanched medallions. *It won't hold,* you say. I hush you as the mortician directs our placement of the casket. We stand outside the tent. The family assumes the draped chairs. I whisper, *The stones will be enough. They said they'd be enough.* Can anything keep such fresh earth still? Someone always presses from below. You think the gravediggers know or can read the dirt etched into the seams of their hands. I think they were there. *Who are those guys who keep passing our windows?* I asked that night. *What guys?* you said, turning your back to the mess on the bed. Even the minister doesn't speak of it but intones words of salvation or some heaven-bound spirit. *She's feeding them dreams,* you whisper. I shift. *No one will know it was you.* You kick at the sod. We're to carry it like we carried the box, no slipping or falling free. *Have a flower*, the minister points to the arranged blooms placed on the box's straps. *Of course,* you say, then wink at me. You take a lily, then let it fall into the depth of the hole. Doesn't anyone recognize this turf, another cheap plastic easy to peel by fingernails? The daughters and their husbands, the grandchildren and the great-grandchildren send more flowers free. Everyone signs the book. I sign. My name curls in black ink, a small claim on the memory we made. You refuse to set yourself to the page, won't even lift the pen. *I'm hungry*, I say. We follow the procession to the church's post-burial meal. Inside, air pots of coffee blink red eyes, the crumbs from wafer cookies scatter, and church ladies spoon meat and gravy over potatoes. We sit across from cousins of cousins of the dead—of her. Everyone swallows their *Whys.* We eat our reasons, choking them down from styrofoam plates. When we rise to find our coats, you say, *The dead are so needy. Why do we think we're done?* I shrug. *Coffin nails were a good tool.* We take the highway from the church, away from the cemetery of restless earth. Faded flags flutter, bitter with the wind.

Stone Clutched to Chest

Held still among crags above the beating shore, bodies surround us. The dark blankets with comfort. I hold him to my chest, stroke his cobbled head, then pat his matted fur. He doesn't know the right shape to be. Why have I forgotten the way? He burbles, coos. His hands flail, red and startled—if they are hands, for already the claws scratch. He runts for a long pull at my emptied teats, but I first feed him congealed blood, thick from the crooks of skulls. Then I crouch over him, sway my six breasts, offer the nipples, waiting for that deep tug of womb to breast, child to cord. Together we curl. Men somewhere pursue us, bearing heavy mail and pride. Waves and wind carry them on laden wood ships, push their flesh and stink toward us. Their songs, drunken melodies of brag or terror, sweep into these caves with promise and threat. I will bare my teeth, then scrape the hearts from their chests to feed the still hot meat to the only one left. For the rest of my children are stones. Once they rose, hunted in the woods, pulled fish from the waters, held berries, bringing that summer sweetness to their lips. Now they have all gone quiet or still. But I feel the thud of my little Grendel's heart, hear his churlish call and its rock-ridden echo. I will not let him join them or leave me to myself. There are moments in this darkness, lit by the fire and reflections of gold when his eyes flutter. The rictus of his mouth widens as if he already knows, the memory of hunt surfacing behind his eyes. I sing to him then, the old songs as he quivers. His limbs twitching a hobbled, jerky dance.

The Path of Coding Eternal

Long after their last breath, the faces of the dead still smile from carefully filtered selfies, the duck faces, days at the beach, nights out with vibrantly colored martinis. Their unself still laughs to a joke long forgotten. Their exes still clutch the necks of bottles, their slim waists, the car keys they should never have held. You think it's weird, the wall-pages of the dead, the tags, pokes, and likes. You think you knew her, even though I didn't know you then. You were still a dishwasher, while I still kneaded dough for the ovens. *I swear I met her at some party,* you insist, scrolling through your tags as if you could place yourself there on the night the jungle juice was spiked with more than what could be found in liquor cabinets. *My sister was dead before we started dating,* I say as you shake your head. After the party, she whore-walked through the morning, mind twisting with what couldn't have happened, but did. When she got home, she shut the cats in the bedroom, then arranged the stack of handwritten notes. She blew out the pilot light, then knelt before the oven's open maw, unsure how else to explain what she carried inside. The timer was set to twenty minutes on the day the woman who came around each week to clean was scheduled to arrive. Did she know that this would be the day the woman would get a flat tire? Before the party, she had tried to erase herself, burning her yearbooks, her photos, her files of taxes and accounting, her memory itself. She couldn't have known how she would linger, still caught in the friends-of-friends feeds, her history filtering through. Bits and bytes of coding call up birthday announcements, anniversary wishes, or party invites—programming still sending love to the lost. Her myspace, the vestibule of a much younger persona, long since forgotten, twitches with life. Her old yahoo email ghosts the group pages. But it's the video of that night, the way it appears, then disappears from sites, that offers fragmented proof of what she must've endured—the twists of flesh, the blood, the sound of them. Why was it never enough? Her last inhale fell to rest, but we read her words that continue clattering through forums and message boards. *Here's another post,* you say. I copy it, as if everything can be saved—the parts of herself she hated or the post-party slurs. I watch for whispers of her each night long after you've gone to sleep. *I would have listened,* I say. *I would have been the one to hold you.* Afraid they'll vanish like her last breath, I copy and paste what I find together.

Holding the Keys

Two dogs ghost my side. They bay at every crossroads,
the four-pronged doorways where I scatter herbs, whisper craft.
The dogs know the passages of the living, the paths of the dead.
I hold the key of many realms, a friend's hand, they their own leash.

In four-pronged doorways I scatter herbs, whisper craft,
draw out poisons, toil for trouble. Under the welkin and moon,
I hold the keys, my friend's cold hand, the dogs their own leash.
Their tongues loll as they lie idle, awaiting their turn.

I draw out poisons, toil for trouble under the welkin and moon
that illuminates the ancient writings of death-lovers and bitches,
while husbands loll, lying idle as they await their turn.
I visit the shrine crowning this city, the marble edifice

that illuminates the ancient writings of death-lovers and bitches,
three-form and moon. This morning, I taste the jeweled fruit left
for my visit of the shrine crowning this city, the marble edifice
a bright egg ready for birthing, heavy with the weight of tides.

The three-form moon floods the morning, as I taste jeweled fruit left
for my arrival. I eclipse a spot on the earth unseen, becoming
a bright egg ready for birthing, heavy with the weight of tides
tethering storms to shores, unleashing the whipping fury of secrets

for my arrival. I eclipse a spot on the earth unseen, becoming
the moon, a friend living in two lands. When to cross? To sacrifice
storms tethered to shores, I unleash a whipping fury of secrets.
Low moans sound as heavy heads and horns strike stone. Bloodied

moon, friend of multiple lands. Where to cross? To sacrifice,
to drape yews over the necks of bulls, burn incense, let smoke rise.
Low moans sound as heavy heads and horns strike bloodied stone.
My names scratch the altar. She prays, lifts hands to shed her shroud

or drape yews over other bulls, burn incense, let smoke rise
to sacrifice the shame of death. When is it enough? Dogs wait, tails
lowered. Our names scratch the altar. She prays to shed her shroud
as I carry the fruit in my hands, bring it to my mouth to lick clean.

Is it enough to wait to sacrifice death's shame? Dogs lower tails.
They know her passages of the living, her paths of the dead.
As I carry her undoing, bringing it to my mouth to lick clean,
two dogs ghost my side—each one baying at the crossroads.

Every Grain of Sand, A Tumbler

To squeeze or tighten, we speak like riddle tellers, guarding sand.
Dried up husks, bones sun-hot, we burden like time. Who figures
this threshold? Which sisters sink beneath the granules

or let river wind grind? Answers puzzle. Questions jumble
our tongue. The path to chart is made of sand. As if this body
of wing and lion claw, beast and living rock could name.

Is my head human, if I kill to eat? Is my flank monstrous, if I'm stone?
Does my claw-pointed crouch clutch at dunes or men who travel?
In solitude, cats, women, and sisters curl together, fur to fur, day to night.

Why do men age? How do sisters give birth to each other?
They carve stories into rock that fail to answer. Inside of me,
there's a temple. Some say it's a tomb. There's a flight of stairs,

walls inscribed in a tongue that not even I can read.
Let silence remain. Wanderers enter, trespass inside
my guardian gut, igniting incense like a curse. It curls,

dissipates until what's left is the feel of deep, wet organs.
Why do they dig into foundations or pry into chambers
to light lamps on forgotten ceremonies that riddle books?

Did our sister wish to throw herself from that rock?
Or did she deny such sacrifice? Did she bare her breast,
pearls at her throat—welcome the priests as they opened

their palms? Or did she savor the heat as it hit her tongue,
burning like the winds of home? To them, we are grotesque,
more bull than cat, more lion than girl. Yet we remain

in stone and sand, our faces chiseled into a mask.
Hunger settled into rock, we question travelers. They believe
as we consume them, it's the flesh that sates,

but we starve for the keys as we swallow their liver
and heart. In our vigil, time churns under our serpent tails' thrash.

Andrea Blythe bides her time waiting for the apocalypse by writing speculative poetry and fiction. Her work has appeared in various publications both online and in print, and has been nominated for a Pushcart Prize, the Rhysling Award, Sundress Best of the Net, and Independent Best American Poetry. She is the author of *Your Molten Heart / A Seed to Hatch*, a collection of erasure poems created from the pages of Trader Joe's Fearless Flyers. She serves as an associate editor for Zoetic Press and is a member of the Science Fiction Poetry Association. Learn more at: www.andreablythe.com

Laura Madeline Wiseman is the author of *Some Fatal Effects of Curiosity and Disobedience* (Lavender Ink), twice nominated for the Elgin Award. Her poetry has appeared in *Strange Horizons, Abyss & Apex, Gingerbread House Literary Magazine, Red Rose Review, Star*Line, Silver Blade*, and elsewhere. Her latest book is *Through a Certain Forest* (BlazeVOX [books] 2017).
Learn more at: www.lauramadelinewiseman.com.